20016271

W9-AAZ-611

AnimalWays

Cheetahs

AnimalWays

Cheetahs

GLORIA G. SCHLAEPFER

BENCHMARK BOOKS

MARSHALL CAVENDISH
NEW YORK

Severn River Media Center

2/7/02

19.95

Green Street

For my grandchildren: Ashley, Isabel, Charles, and Johannes
—G. G. S.

Thank you to Susan Millard at the San Diego Wild Animal Park for the extensive interview she gave me. And deep appreciation to all the wildlife biologists whose research and writings provide us with in-depth knowledge of the cheetah and other wild animals.

With thanks to Dr. Dan Wharton, director of the Central Park Wildlife Center, for his expert reading of this manuscript.

Benchmark Books
Marshall Cavendish Corporation
99 White Plains Road
Tarrytown, NY 10591-9001
Website: www.marshallcavendish.com

Text copyright © 2002 by Gloria G. Schlaepfer
Illustrations copyright © 2002 by Ka Botzis
Map by Carol Matsuyama
Map copyright © 2002 by Marshall Cavendish Corporation

Library of Congress Cataloging-in-Publication Data
Schlaepfer, Gloria G.
Cheetahs / by Gloria G. Schlaepfer.
p. cm. — (Animal ways)
Includes bibliographical references (p. 107) and index (p. 109)
ISBN 0-7614-1266-2
1.Cheetah—Juvenile literature. [1. Cheetah.] I. Title. II. Animal ways (Tarrytown, N.Y.)
QL737.C23 S343 2001 599.75'9—dc21 00-050738

Photo Research by Candlepants Incorporated

Cover Photo: Photo Researchers, Inc./Leonard Lee Rue III

The photographs in this book are used by permission and through the courtesy of: *Gerry Ellis/ENP Images*: 2, 18, 35, 58, 63, 79, 93, 98,100; *Animals Animals*: Norbert Rosing OSF, 9, 84; Betty H. Press, 38; Robert Winslow, 39, 42; J. Downer OSF, 50-51; Joe McDonald, 57, 87 (lower); David Breed OSF, 68, 75; Anup Shah, 71, 74, back cover; Michael Fogden, 86 (lower); D. Allen, 86 (upper); Peter Weimann, 87 (upper); Mitch Reardon, 89; Rick Edwards, 104; *Photo Researchers, Inc*: Tom Brakefield, 11, 75; J.H. Blower, 13; Anthony Bannester,14; Tom McHugh, 23; M.P. Kail, 32; Stephen J. Krasemann, 44, 83; Ron Austing, 45; Ann Purcell, 53; Adam Jones, 55; Leonard Lee Rue III, 60; Clem Haagner, 66-67; Art Wolfe, 70. *Victoria & Albert Museum/Art Resource NY*: 16; *Denver Museum of Nature and Science/Rick Wicker*: 24; *Corbis*: Michael & Patricia Fogden, 96.

Printed in Italy

1 3 5 6 4 2

Contents

HERE ARE SOME OF THE MAIN PHYLA, CLASSES, AND ORDERS, WITH PHOTOGRAPHS OF
A TYPICAL ANIMAL FROM EACH GROUP.

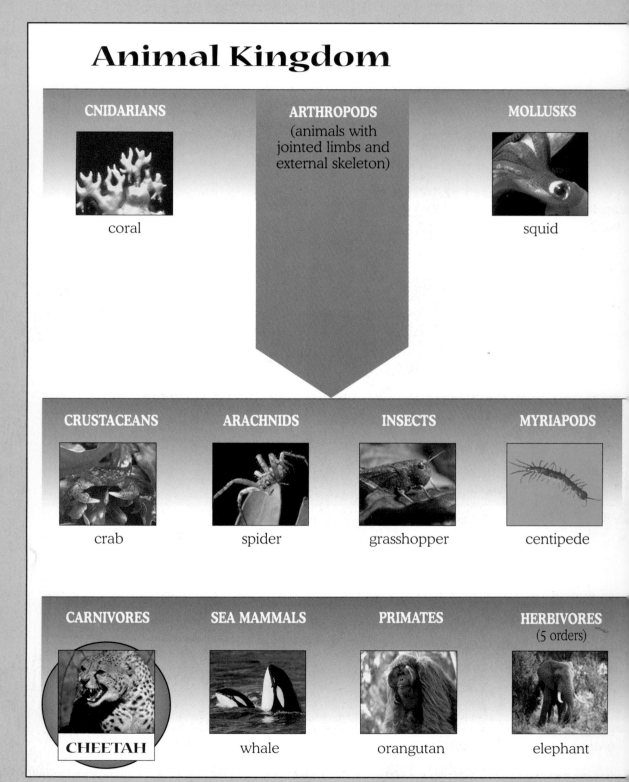

Animal Kingdom

CNIDARIANS

coral

ARTHROPODS
(animals with
jointed limbs and
external skeleton)

MOLLUSKS

squid

CRUSTACEANS

crab

ARACHNIDS

spider

INSECTS

grasshopper

MYRIAPODS

centipede

CARNIVORES

CHEETAH

SEA MAMMALS

whale

PRIMATES

orangutan

HERBIVORES
(5 orders)

elephant

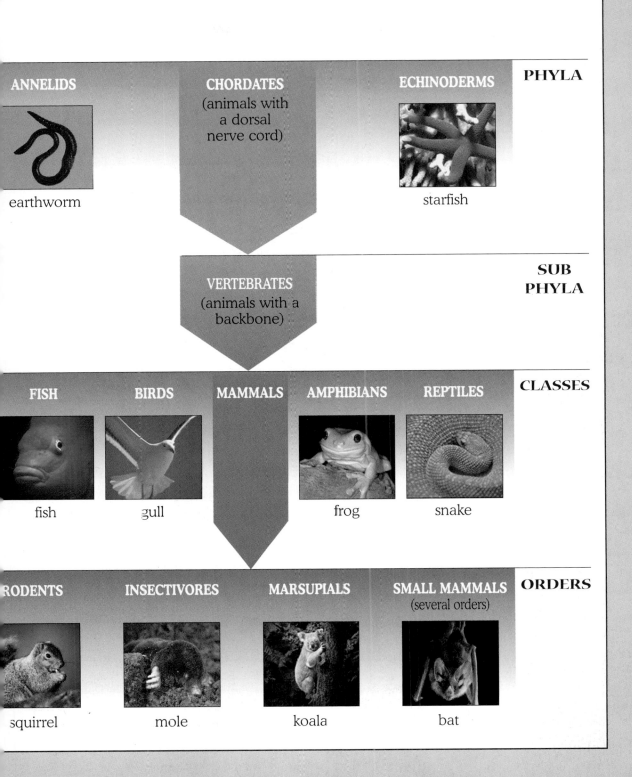

PHYLA

ANNELIDS

earthworm

CHORDATES
(animals with
a dorsal
nerve cord)

ECHINODERMS

starfish

SUB PHYLA

VERTEBRATES
(animals with a
backbone)

CLASSES

FISH

fish

BIRDS

gull

MAMMALS

AMPHIBIANS

frog

REPTILES

snake

ORDERS

RODENTS

squirrel

INSECTIVORES

mole

MARSUPIALS

koala

SMALL MAMMALS
(several orders)

bat

1 The World of Cheetahs

On a bright, warm morning, a mother cheetah rests inside a tangle of thorny shrubs. Her four tiny, newborn cubs nestle beside her. They press their little faces deeply into her soft fur. The mother has not eaten for many days, and she is hungry. She rises, stretches her legs, and starts to walk. The cubs, startled by their mother's sudden movement, whimper softly. The mother cheetah turns and utters a soft, churring sound to them: Stay quiet and still. The cubs hunt around until they find one another. They huddle together for warmth and comfort. Their mother leaves them and moves cautiously through the tangled branches to a clearing. She sniffs the air and looks carefully for any hint of danger. When she is satisfied that it is safe to leave her young cubs, she walks away.

The open grassland stretches before her. In the distance, the cheetah sees zebras, Thomson's gazelles, and wildebeests grazing calmly. She crouches to hide. Her slim body and spotted coat

DURING THEIR FIRST MONTHS, CHEETAH CUBS GET ALL THE FOOD THEY NEED FROM THEIR MOTHER'S MILK.

blend into the tawny grasses. The top of her head is barely visible.

The cheetah moves directly toward the herd with slow, cautious steps. The gazelles remain alert and raise their heads often to look around. Each time they do, the cheetah freezes, motionless. When the gazelles lower their heads again to eat, she moves forward. The cheetah stares intently at the herd—not even the biting flies distract her. Her plan is to watch, creep a little closer, and wait for the right moment to attack.

Many minutes pass. When the cheetah is within one hundred feet (30.5 meters) of the herd, she sprints toward it. The wildebeests, zebras, and gazelles scatter wildly in all directions. The cheetah focuses her attention on one of the fleeing gazelles and gallops after it. As panic seizes the gazelle, it runs, jumps, twists, and turns back and forth. The gazelle is no match for the cheetah, which moves at lightning speed. With huge strides and focused attention, the cheetah overtakes the gazelle, swatting its hind legs with her front paw to knock it down. As the animal falls, the cheetah jumps onto its back and neck. In a flash, she grabs the gazelle by the throat and closes her jaws on its windpipe. The gazelle's body soon goes limp.

Breathing heavily, the cheetah sits down next to the gazelle's body to rest. When she has regained her strength, she drags her prey to a clump of bushes. She eats quickly, stopping every few minutes to sit up and look for prowling lions or soaring vultures that might steal her meal. Hours later, she returns to her cubs. Licking their faces, she reassures them that all is well.

The Spotted Cat

Cheetahs are unique among the large cats. They are the Olympic champions of the animal world. Over short distances, cheetahs are the fastest land animals, able to run up to sixty-five

THIS CHEETAH IS CARRYING ITS KILL TO A SAFE SPOT BEFORE EATING IT.

to seventy miles (104 to 112 kilometers) per hour. Within seconds, they can leap from a crouching position into a sprinting speed of forty-five miles (72 km) per hour and then quickly accelerate to full speed. An incredible feat for any animal! The cheetah's body is built for speed. It has long, thin, muscular legs, a narrow waist, a deep chest with large lungs, wide nasal cavities, and blunt claws—all of which help the animal move fast.

The common name *cheetah* is from the Hindu word *chita*, which means "the spotted one." Its short, coarse coat ranges from tawny to pale buff or grayish white on the cheetah's back, with a white underside. Each cheetah has its own distinctive pattern of spots. Halfway down the tail, the spots blend together to form stripes. The tail has a white tip. A cheetah's face gets its characteristic appearance from the black stripe resembling a teardrop that extends from the inside corner of its eye to its mouth. The stripe may help block the glare from the sun—just as black liner under the eyes does for football players.

The cheetah's scientific name is *Acinonyx jubatus*. The word *Acinonyx* is from the Greek word *akaina*, meaning "thorn," and *onyx*, meaning "claw." *Jubatus* is from the Latin word that refers to the mane found in cheetah cubs and some adults. This animal's hair is slightly longer at the neck, forming the short mane.

Early in the twentieth century, cheetahs with a rare coat pattern were found in southern Africa. These animals, called king cheetahs, had longer, softer fur than other cheetahs. Some of their black spots blended together into bars or stripes. Scientists disagreed about this creature. Some felt that this animal was the same species as the spotted cheetah known as *Acinonyx jubatus*. They believed it was simply a cheetah with an unusual color pattern. Others thought that these African cheetahs were members of a new species, *Acinonyx rex*, or "king cheetah." In the 1980s, two cheetah cubs were born with the same rare striped coat. Both of the cubs' parents were spotted cheetahs. That was the proof. Scientists then learned that the king cheetah is a spotted cheetah with a different fur texture and pattern.

Acinonyx jubatus is the only surviving species of the genus *Acinonyx*. Along with the thirty-seven other cat species, *Acinonyx*

TWO PROMINENT BLACK STRIPES RUN LIKE TEARS DOWN A CHEETAH'S FACE.

THE KING CHEETAH'S BLACK SPOTS BLEND TOGETHER TO CREATE BOLD, DRAMATIC PATTERNS.

jubatus belongs to the cat family Felidae. The cheetah—just like all of its felid relatives—is a carnivorous, or meat-eating, mammal that hunts for its food.

Unlike the other big cats, cheetahs usually hunt during the day. They rely mainly on their vision to select an animal as their prey. Then they pursue the animal in a very fast chase. Because of their spotted coats and their special hunting style, cheetahs were sometimes called "hunting leopards."

Early in history, humans recognized the cheetah's unique abilities. People also soon discovered that even adult cheetahs could be tamed. A cheetah is probably the only large cat that can be removed from the wild and tamed easily. After a wild cheetah was caught, the trainer would begin to offer the cat small amounts of food. Slowly, the animal would lose its natural aggression and eat directly from the trainer's hand. A tame cheetah can be walked like a dog, held in check by a leash.

For more than four centuries, in Asia and Africa, cheetahs were trapped, tamed, and trained to be hunting companions for people—much as dogs are today. The royal rulers in ancient Egypt, Sumeria, and Assyria, as well as the Mogul princes in India used cheetahs in the hunting sport called coursing. In coursing, hunters pursue game animals with the help of other animals. As the hunting parties set out, the cheetah's head was covered with a hood to so that the animal couldn't see. As soon as game was spotted, the cheetah's hood was removed, and the cat was released. After a successful hunt, the cheetah was rewarded with parts of the dead animal.

In 1884, R. A. Sterndale wrote about this practice. He explained that, if the cheetah killed a male antelope, it was permitted to eat the prey's hind legs. The cheetah was then gently pulled away so the hunters could remove the prey animal's internal organs. The organs were given to the cheetah in a special

IN THIS INDIAN
PAINTING FROM
ABOUT 1600,
MOGUL PRINCE
AKBAR AND HIS
HUNTING PARTY
USE TRAINED
CHEETAHS TO
BRING DOWN
GAME.

bowl. If the cheetah killed a female antelope, however, it would not receive any of the meat, as a punishment. After six months, the cheetah learned to select only male prey—for which it would be rewarded with food. If a cheetah tried to escape, hunters on horseback easily recaptured it, as the cat lacks stamina and tires easily after running a short distance.

Coursing became very popular after the sixteenth century. Cheetahs were found in the hunting lodges of Turkish sultans and German emperors. Akbar the Great, Mogul emperor of India from 1556 to 1605, kept a stable of more than one thousand cheetahs to hunt antelope. The emperor tried to breed the cheetahs, but was unsuccessful. So, cheetahs continued to be trapped and imported from their natural habitats in southwest Asia and North Africa.

Cheetah Country

Cheetahs need large, open lands for their high-speed chases after their prey. The vast grassland and savanna belt of Africa, south of the Sahara, is ideal. The region lies north and south of the equator between the tropic of Cancer and the tropic of Capricorn. The broad belt extends from Senegal to southern Somalia, Kenya, and Tanzania. It then stretches south from Angola, western Zambia, and Namibia to South Africa.

The gently rolling plains extend as far as the eye can see. The plant growth varies throughout this extensive landscape. Almost everywhere, low-growing grasses cover the soil. In areas with more rainfall, savannas and woodlands develop. A savanna is a grassland with scattered bushy shrubs and trees, such as the umbrella-shaped acacia trees or the large sausage trees. The grasslands and savannas may abruptly turn to woodlands, where feather-leafed shrubs, with their long spines, spread in place of

grasses. In some parts of the plains, there are quiet pools of water, rivers, and streams. Here, fever trees, wild date palms, and fig trees can be found growing. Cheetahs need both the grasslands and the wooded habitats: the open grasslands as a hunting ground and the woodlands as a safe hiding place from enemies and the blistering hot sun.

The types of plants and where they grow in the grasslands are determined by several factors: elevation, temperature, rainfall, the seasons, and the grazing animals. There is some grassland along the coast, but most of the belt is in eastern, central, and southern Africa. These areas sit on high plateaus that are 3,000 to 5,000 feet (900 to 1,500 m) in elevation. There are also mountain ranges and some isolated mountains in the region. The volcanic Mount Kilimanjaro, Africa's tallest mountain, reaches to 19,340 feet (5,895 meters).

The area's climate is greatly affected by the presence of the mountains and mountain ranges. As moisture-carrying winds encounter a mountain, the air rises and cools. Cool air holds less moisture than warm air, so the cool air then drops its moisture load in the form of rain, fog, or snow onto the mountainside. When the wind descends on the opposite side, or lee side, of the mountain, the air becomes warmer and is able to hold more moisture. Rather than dropping rain or snow, the warm air instead draws moisture

BURCHELL'S ZEBRAS MOVE ACROSS THE VAST SERENGETI PLAIN.

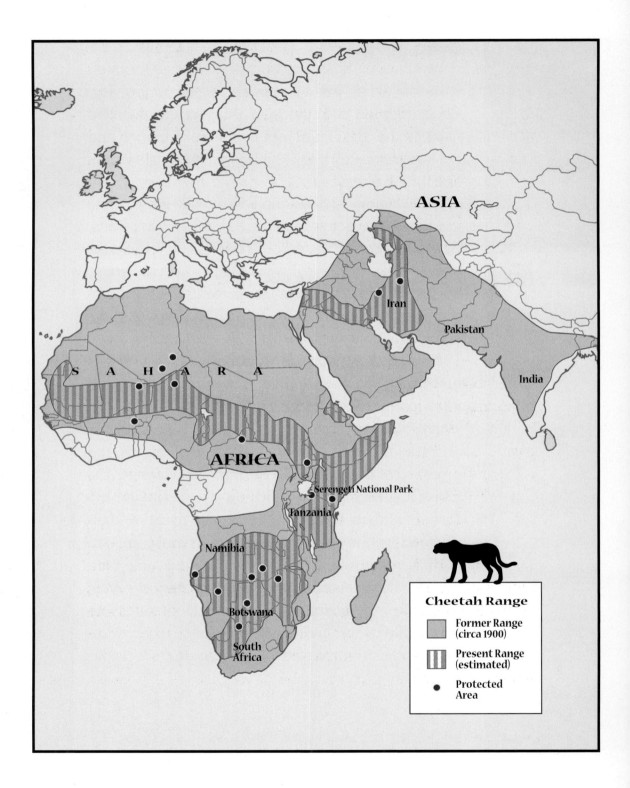

ASIA

Iran

Pakistan

India

S A H A R A

AFRICA

Serengeti National Park

Tanzania

Namibia

Botswana

South
Africa

Cheetah Range

Former Range
(circa 1900)

Present Range
(estimated)

Protected
Area

from the soil and the plants. The result on the lee side of the mountain is a much drier landscape, and, in some places, deserts.

Even without the influence of mountains, the rainfall varies throughout the grassland and savanna belt. In the coastal, low-elevation areas at the equator, it rains often, and the weather is warm and humid for most of the year. On the high-plateau north and south of the equator, between the tropics of Cancer and Capricorn, the rainfall is more moderate and less frequent. One or two wet seasons a year provide the region with twelve to thirty-five inches (300 to 900 mm) of rainfall. A long, dry season follows the rainy seasons. During the dry season, temperatures rise. When the rains return, milder temperatures also return, and the high-plateau areas are again covered with grasses.

The rainfall maintains the long, narrow lakes and swells the rivers to overflowing. It fills the water holes that animals use to drink and wallow or bathe in. Rain makes it possible for nutritious grasses to sprout two to three feet (60 to 90 centimeters) in height. The trees leaf out, flowers envelop the branches, and fruits follow. The grasses and the leaves, fruits, and seed pods of trees and shrubs attract and feed a great variety of wildlife. This region is home to the highest concentration of ungulates— hoofed mammals—in the world.

The grasslands are kept intact by the constant grazing of those animals. The herds of buffalo, wildebeests, zebras, and antelopes act like lawn mowers as they cut and chew the grasses and the emerging shoots of shrubs and trees. Elephants sometimes knock down trees and pull out bushy shrubs to reach the plant's green leaves. Without these grazers, the grasslands would soon grow into woodlands and forests.

2 Prehistoric Relatives

To better understand how cheetahs and other cats look and act the way they do, we need to look way back in time and trace their evolution. Evolution is a gradual process by which living organisms change over millions of years. It is not a straight or smooth line, but is often marked by fits and starts. New species develop; others die out.

Animals, as well as all living organisms, are influenced by many factors. They respond to changes in climate and to predation. They compete with other species for available resources such as food and space. The primary forces behind evolution, however, are mutation and natural selection.

Mutation occurs when there is a change in the characteristic of an organism. That change is passed on by the genes of a parent to its young and then on to future generations. Genes are the tiny units of a cell that carry the characteristics. For example,

THE BONES AND TEETH OF THIS SABER-TOOTHED CAT ARE A WELL-PRESERVED FOSSIL SPECIMEN.

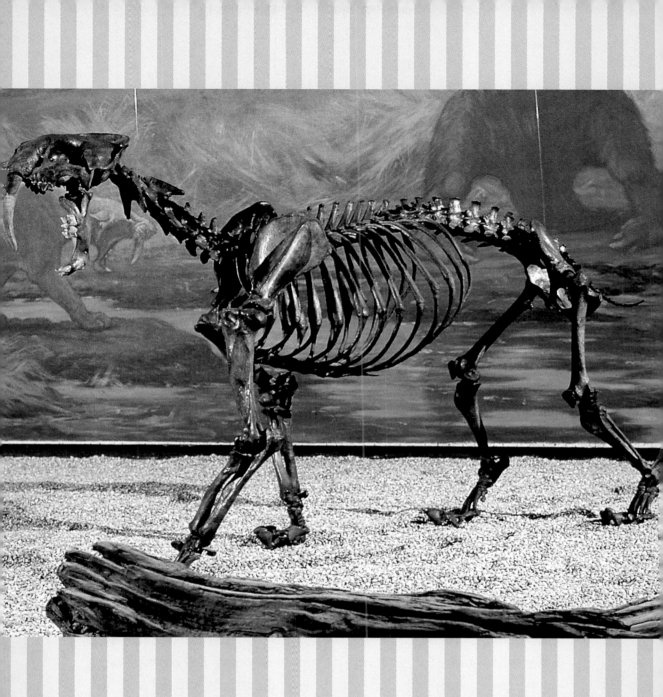

the wings of houseflies may become larger over time. If the changed flies adapt or function better than their parents, they are more apt to survive and produce their own young. This process is called natural selection. The new organism is "selected" by nature and will gradually replace the original organism. It will take many, many years, perhaps millions, for those small changes to result in a new species.

Fossils provide a record of those changes. Fossils are the traces of an organism that have been preserved. Parts of a plant or animal that lived thousands or millions of years ago may have hardened into rock, or become fossilized. Because flesh or the other soft parts of the body decays, only bones, teeth, woody plants, and shells become fossilized. Sometimes, a footprint or an impression of a body or a plant is also found in the earth. Paleontologists—scientists who study prehistoric living organisms—compare fossils with modern species. The paleontologist can then put together a picture of the life-forms in that prehistoric period of time. The fossil record is often scanty, however, so scientists must work with bits and pieces to find the answers.

The Evolution of Mammals

The evolution of mammals began about 275 million years ago, in the time known as the early Permian period. Life on Earth was quite different then. The continents formed one giant super-continent called Pangaea. The climate was dry and seasonal. Evergreen trees with cones and bladelike leaves, primitive seed plants, and feathery-leafed ferns were abundant. A diverse group of mammal-like reptiles, called protomammals, flourished then. These creatures were more like reptiles than mammals—but they were the first link between reptiles and true mammals.

For 100 million years, protomammals adapted to the different

The fossilized skeletal remains of *Dimetrodon limbatus*, a fin-backed protomammal, and *Eryops megacephalus*, the big-headed amphibian, commonly appear in rocks from the Permian period, 275 million years ago.

climates and landscapes of the changing Earth. Some of these animals could partly control their internal body temperature. This trait marked the shift from the cold-bloodedness of reptiles to the warm-bloodedness of mammals. One group, the therapsids, may even have had fur on their bodies to help them cope with the cold winters. Another group of protomammals was the cynodonts. They were small and pursued insect prey. They hid in holes or under bushes to avoid the hot sun and larger predators.

The herbivorous, or plant-eating, therapsids looked like small buffalo. The carnivorous species, called the theriodonts, grew to the size of large bears. Instead of the sharp bladelike teeth of a reptile, theriodonts had teeth that resembled those of modern mammals. During this period, however, large carnivorous reptiles dominated the environment. About 230 million years ago, the earlier forms of reptiles began to be replaced by dinosaurs, pterosaurs, ichthyosaurs, lizards, and the crocodiles. The once-widespread protomammals vanished from Earth about 160 million years ago. The cynodonts vanished, too, but were the ancestors of the true mammals.

During the next 100 million years—known as the Upper Cretaceous Period—mammals were mouse-sized animals that were able to adapt to life with the dinosaurs and other giants. *Morganucondon* was only four inches (10 cm) long and weighed about one ounce (28 grams). Its fossilized skeleton reveals that it could climb and run quickly. These nocturnal, insect-eating mammals lived in niches hidden from the dinosaurs.

Throughout the Cretaceous period, continents shifted, and new forms of both plants and animals evolved. At the end of the period—about 65 million years ago—the dinosaurs, marine reptiles, and flying reptiles that had ruled the Earth, seas, and sky became extinct. Because they were no longer being hunted by these creatures, mammals thrived. Within 1 million years, the number of mammalian families increased from twelve to nearly 120. Mammals became the dominant species on Earth. Amazing, when you realize it took 20 million years to get from the earliest protomammals to this stage in mammalian evolution!

These early mammals were small to medium in size. Among them were plant eaters, anteaters, and meat eaters. There were two groups of meat eaters: the carnivorans and the creodonts. The bear-size creodonts, with long legs for running down prey, were fierce predators. They had powerful jaws, well-developed canine teeth, and special cheek teeth for shearing, or slicing, the flesh of their victims. Despite their hunting prowess, the creodonts died out 40 million years ago.

While the creodonts reigned, the ancestors of the modern carnivores emerged: a small group of catlike animals, called miacids, in the superfamily *Miacoidea*. The miacids were small, short-legged animals with long bodies and tails, much like today's pine martens. Their wide paws, which had spreading, grasping fingers and toes, suggest that they lived in trees. Scientists believe that miacids inhabited the forests of the Northern Hemisphere from 60 to 39 million years ago.

During the next 20 million years an unusually rapid evolution took place. From it, the modern families of the order *Carnivora* emerged. One group, the arctoids, included bears, pandas, dogs, raccoons, badgers, skunks, weasels, and seals. The other group, the aeluroids, included the cats, genets, civets, mongooses, and hyenas. Both of these groups had scissorlike shearing teeth and hingelike jaw joints. In addition, they both typically had fused wrist bones and a modified collarbone. The groups had two significant differences, however. Unlike the bear group, the cat group had an internal, bony wall protecting the tympanic bulla, a large chamber of the middle ear. Second, all members of the cat group had retractile or semiretractile claws—which meant that these animals could draw their claws into their paws to conceal them. Modern cats have all of the unique physical features of the aeluroids.

True Cats Appear

Two lines of cats evolved from the primitive cats: the paleofelids and the neofelids. The paleofelids, or false saber-toothed cats, appeared 37 to 24 million years ago. The neofelids, or true cats, from the family *Felidae*, appeared about 25 million years ago. All modern cats are placed in two subfamilies of the *Felidae* family: *Felinae* and *Pantherinae*. Also included are various forms of saber-toothed cats, all extinct. One of the last to appear was *Smilodon fatalis*. This cat is best known for its six-inch- (15-cm-) long canine teeth and from the large number of its fossilized bones found in Rancho La Brea Tar Pits in Los Angeles, California.

Scientists disagree about the evolutionary pathway of modern cats. Part of the reason is the lack of complete skeletons from ancestral cats. Many of these animals lived in forested lands, and their remains were less likely to be preserved. Because of advances in technology, however, scientists can study evolution in the laboratory. To track the history of cats, they now focus on genetic material—deoxyribonucleic acid (DNA). DNA controls the activities of cells in the body. It also transmits the characteristics of a species from one generation to the next.

In one laboratory study, geneticist Steven O'Brien compared the DNA of all living cat species by using blood and skin cell samples. He concluded that there are three major evolutionary lines of the *Felidae* family. The first line from the ancestral cats appeared about twelve million years ago. It led to the

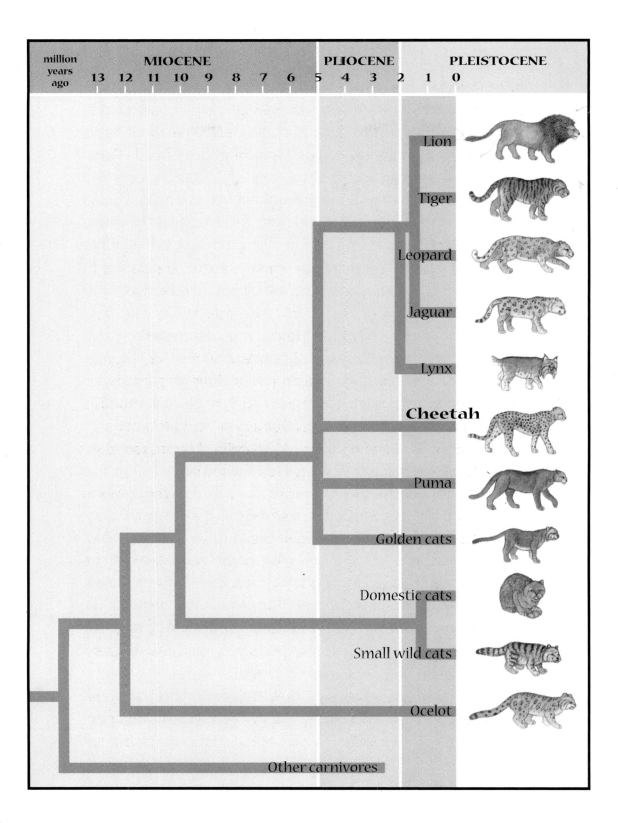

million years ago	MIOCENE								PLIOCENE				PLEISTOCENE		
	13	12	11	10	9	8	7	6	5	4	3	2	1	0	

Lion

Tiger

Leopard

Jaguar

Lynx

Cheetah

Puma

Golden cats

Domestic cats

Small wild cats

Ocelot

Other carnivores

ocelot, margay, and other cats now found in South America. The second line evolved two million years later and included the Old World species of small wild cats. In the next four to six million years, the middle-sized and large cats developed. These represent all the cats in the *Pantherine* line. The big cats and lynxes split off from that branch about two to four million years ago. Before the DNA studies, scientists believed that the cheetah separated from the common ancestral line about eight million years ago. Now scientists know that the cheetah is in the *Pantherine* group, along with the other middle-sized and large cats.

During the last two million years, the ancestors of the cheetah were widely dispersed throughout the world. Of the four cheetah-like cats that once existed, only *Acinonyx jubatus* has survived. *Acinonyx pardinensis*, which weighed twice as much as *Acinonyx jubatus*, lived in Europe two to four million years ago. A smaller species, *Acinonyx intermedius*, ranged from Europe to China. Two large cats, *Miracinonyx studeri* and *Miracinonyx trumani* lived in North America during the late Pleistocene era, about 1.6 million years ago. The two species had physical characteristics that matched those of *Acinonyx jubatus*. They had small, domed heads with enlarged nasal cavities—features found in running cats. Their upper canine teeth were small, again similar to *Acinonyx jubatus*. For these and various other reasons, some scientists believe *Miracinonyx* and *Acinonyx* are related and that they share a common ancestor. These findings called the origin of cheetahs into question.

Other scientists proposed that the similarities between *Miracinonyx* and *Acinonyx* are the result of convergent evolution. Plants or animals that have evolved in the same environmental conditions—even in separate areas or continents—may resemble one another but still have different ancestors. In additional studies, including genetic tests of cheetahs and cougars, scientists later determined that the two extinct North American running cats are in the separate genus *Miracinonyx*.

Modern Cheetahs

Ten thousand years ago, the last Ice Age ended. The large animals of the forests and prairies—including the giant sloths, saber-toothed cats, and mastodons—became extinct. Most of the cheetahs died out, too, although somehow a few persisted. Slowly, during the next ten thousand years, the cheetah population rebounded from those few survivors. As a result of this inbreeding—mating only within a small group of related individuals—the cheetah population shows little genetic difference between individuals. They are as similar to one another as twins. Nevertheless, cheetahs multiplied and spread across Africa and the Middle East and into parts of Asia and India.

Today, scientists recognize five subspecies of cheetahs. Each one shows a slight difference in physical characteristics from *Acinonyx jubatus*. The subspecies *Acinonyx jubatus jubatus* is found in South Africa. *Acinonyx jubatus raineyii* is found in East Africa. *Acinonyx jubatus soemmeringii* lives in Sudan, and *Acinonyx jubatus hecki* in northwest Africa. *Acinonyx jubatus venaticus* is found in India and North Africa.

According to some estimates, there may have been as many as 100,000 cheetahs in the world in 1900. They ranged throughout North Africa, the plains of central Africa, and southwestern Asia from Iran to India. In recent years, the cheetah population has declined greatly. Today, there may be no more than ten thousand of these animals worldwide. They are restricted to the savannas and semidesert areas south of the Sahara: East Africa, Namibia, Botswana, Zimbabwe, and South Africa. A

During the day, cheetahs remain alert as they search for food and watch for predators.

tiny population may still exist or be on the verge of extinction in Iran and northwest Afghanistan.

Cheetahs are in trouble. Many factors threaten their survival: disease and natural predators, loss of natural habitats, and poachers and other people who hunt them for skins and as trophies. As a result, cheetahs have been classified as an endangered species by the Conservation of International Trade in Endangered Species (CITES). Cheetahs have been part of our natural world for millions of years. Through efforts to educate people and protect the animals, cheetahs can remain a part of our world for a long time to come. Let's take a closer look now at this beautiful felid.

3 The Cheetah, Inside and Out

S ome people think the cheetah is the strangest-looking of the big cats. Others wonder if the animal is really half dog and half cat. This feline is easily distinguished from other cats by its long, lanky body. Its small, domed head has high-set eyes and small, rounded ears. Its face has distinctive black tear lines.

The cheetah is considered a medium-sized cat. Although cheetahs and leopards weigh about the same, the cheetah has a longer body and longer legs. A cheetah's slender body and head measure 45 to 54 inches (112 to 135 cm) in length, and its long tail adds another 26 to 34 inches (66 to 84 cm). An adult cheetah may weigh from 55 to143 pounds (25 to 64 kilograms). Males generally are longer and heavier than females. A robust lion may be more than three times heavier than a cheetah and twice as long.

THE LARGE, POWERFUL CHEST AND SMALL, DOMED HEAD DISTINGUISH THIS STALKING CHEETAH.

Built for Speed

The cheetah is a champion sprinter. If all the land animals had a foot race, the cheetah would win the first-place prize. Just how fast can a cheetah run? Estimates vary from sixty miles (96 km) per hour to more than eighty miles (128 km) per hour. The cheetah's racing speed has been clocked with a stopwatch as the animal covered a known distance—from point A to point B. Cheetahs have even raced against greyhounds on a dog-racing track. Zoologist Milton Hildebrand filmed a running cheetah and analyzed its high-speed movements. The studies show that cheetahs can run at least seventy miles per hour (110 km) for a short distance. That's faster than horses and dogs can run—and faster than antelopes, the cheetah's favorite prey.

The cheetah's athletic body is finely tuned for maximum performance. It has evolved for speed, rather than for climbing or strength: long muscular legs, an agile torso, flexible backbone, long tail, and blunt claws. The long legs and flexible spine increase the length of the animal's stride—the distance traveled in a long step. The shoulder bone is longer in a cheetah than it is in most cats. The lower end of the shoulder joint is free to move forward and back with the swing of the leg, which also increases the cheetah's stride. The cheetah's long tail with its twenty-eight vertebrae, or small bones, provides balance while the animal is running at top speed. The tail also helps the cat to quickly switch directions or make sharp turns as it pursues its prey.

Like other cats, a cheetah walks and runs on its toes. Because only the toes touch the ground, the cheetah exerts less energy when running, and its stride length increases, too. The blunt claws on each of the cheetah's toes dig into the ground like the cleats on a runner's shoes. They help prevent the cat from slipping while it's running and turning. The padded toe

Cheetah Skeleton

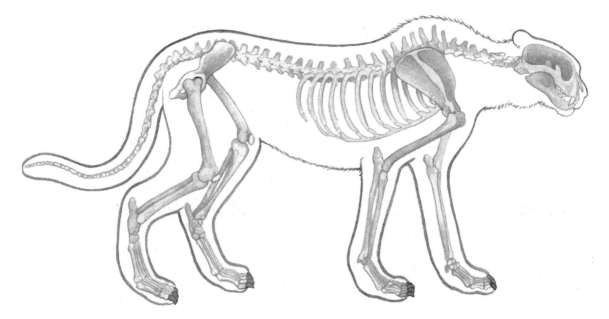

cushions help the body absorb the shock of the pounding that naturally occurs when running. The pads on a cheetah's toes are thicker than most cats' toe pads. They also contain ridges or grooves. The ridges provide extra traction as the animal moves—working in much the same way as treads on the tires of a car. The bones in the feet, ankles, and legs are stabilized to provide strength when the animal pushes off to sprint forward.

As the chase begins, the muscular hind legs push against the ground and propel the animal forward in a sprint. The cat then moves faster, using the legs on one side of the body first and then the other. Strong back and chest muscles provide extra power. In two seconds, the cheetah is running at forty-five miles (55 km) per hour. Then, it breaks into a gallop. Now, the muscular hind legs work in unison. They press down together for greater forward thrust, while the forelegs touch down alternately. As the

BEGINNING ITS RUN, THIS CHEETAH SPRINGS FORWARD BY USING ITS POWERFUL BACK LEGS.

cheetah gathers speed, its long body and legs stretch out in long strides. The fast-moving cat appears to float above the ground.

In its final burst of speed, the hind legs flex up under the forelegs and the chest. They then extend down and back in one powerful motion. Then, the forelegs extend forward and pull back—a movement similar to the arms of a swimmer doing the breaststroke. A cheetah can travel a phenomenal twenty-three

A CHEETAH'S LONG TAIL HELPS THE CAT TO KEEP ITS BALANCE WHEN RUNNING AT TOP SPEED.

feet (7 meters) in one stride. An average chase after prey may last no more than thirty seconds. In that short time, the cheetah may cover more than 400 to 600 yards (364 to 546 m) before becoming too exhausted to continue.

During this high-speed chase, lots of energy is used to fuel those muscles and the muscles of the heart. The key to energy is oxygen. As the animal inhales, it takes oxygen into its lungs,

Cheetah Organs

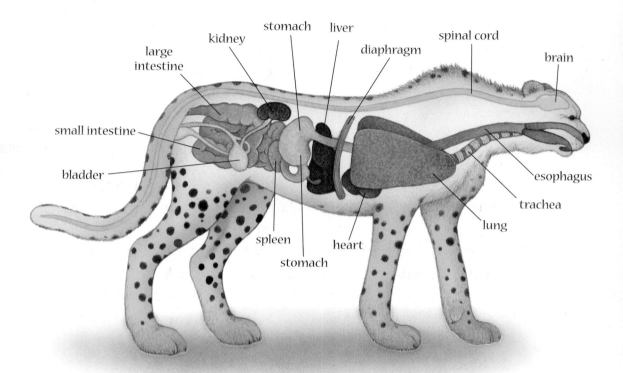

which is then passed into the blood. The heart then pumps the oxygen-rich blood to all parts of the body. The cheetah's four-chambered heart is small but it performs awesome work.

To allow the animal to take as much air as possible into its lungs, the cheetah has large nasal cavities and a wide trachea, or windpipe. The extra oxygen it takes into its lungs fuels the work-ing muscles and also aids in heavy breathing. The large nasal cav-ities also make it possible for the exhausted cheetah to breathe through its nose while it holds the prey's throat in its mouth.

Teeth and Digestion

When the prey animal has been killed, the teeth go to work. Cheetahs and other cats have fewer teeth than other carnivorous mammals. They have approximately thirty: sixteen in the upper jaw and fourteen in the lower jaw. In contrast, a gray wolf may have as many as forty-two teeth.

The various types of cat teeth have specific functions. The six, small, incisor teeth, which are arranged in a straight row at the front of the jaw, are used to remove the last bits of meat from bones. Next to the incisors are the large, round, pointed fangs, or canine teeth, which are found at the corners of the mouth. When a cat opens its mouth, those are the teeth that are most noticeable. Most cats use their canine teeth to hold their prey and inflict the deadly bite to the animal's spinal cord. The cheetah's canines, however, are shorter and smaller than other cats', and it does not bite to kill. A cheetah uses its canines to hold the prey by the throat in order to suffocate it.

Farther back in the cheetah's jaws, the scissorlike molars, or carnassials, rip and chew chunks of flesh from the *carcass*, or dead body. The carnassials are a distinctive set of teeth formed by the cheek teeth. The sharp tips and jagged edges of the last upper premolar and first lower molar fit perfectly together to form the set. The cheetah's carnassials are especially narrow. Scientists believe that these teeth are small to allow more space in the skull for the expanded nasal cavities. Working against each other, these teeth slice flesh or cut through tough tendons. The cheetah swallows the large chunks of meat whole.

The cheetah does not need to open its jaws as wide as other cats do to bite, so the cheetah's gape, or size of its open mouth, is smaller than most cats'. The jaw joint is also hinged so that it moves up and down. This movement of the jaw allows the

The open mouth of this snarling cheetah shows the animal's sharp canine teeth.

cheetah's carnassials to cut against one another, like the blades of a pair of scissors. In contrast, the jaws of plant-eating animals move in a side-to-side motion as their teeth crush and grind food into small pieces.

Large and powerful muscles on each side of a cheetah's skull enable the animal's jaws to open and close. The strong chewing muscles provide the strength the animal needs to clamp its jaws shut and hold its struggling prey in a viselike grip. The supporting muscles form a strong hinge that permits only one pair of carnassial teeth to chew at a time. Cats chew on one side of their mouths before switching to the other side—which is why cats tilt their heads while eating.

A cheetah uses its incisor teeth—and its tongue—to scrape off the last bits of meat from the bones of its prey. Have you ever noticed the rough, prickly bumps that make a cat's tongue feel like sandpaper? The rough surface is caused by tiny backward-pointing hooks called papillae.

All cats mainly eat flesh. In this way, they differ from other carnivores, such as dogs and bears, which sometimes also eat and digest plant food. Plant matter requires greater digestion. Because the cheetah eats only meat, its stomach is a simple pouch. Its large intestine is shorter and has fewer folds than that of plant-eating animals. The meat, which is rich in protein, moves easily through the cat's simple digestive tract. Powerful enzymes and acids then break down the protein so that the animal's body can use it as fuel.

The cheetah also uses its tongue to groom its fur. Cats do not bathe in water but they are among the cleanest animals. Several times a day, a cheetah may lick its paws or use its tongue to wipe dried blood and dirt from its face and head. Then, it uses its raspy tongue like a hairbrush to remove dirt and loose hairs from the rest of its coat.

WHILE RESTING TOGETHER, CHEETAHS CLEAN EACH OTHER'S FACES WITH THEIR RASPY TONGUES.

The Senses

Daytime hunters like cheetahs depend on their acute eyesight to hunt successfully. The animal's round forward-facing eyes have binocular, or stereoscopic, vision. With this type of vision, the two eyes work together so the cheetah can accurately judge the distance between itself and its prey before beginning the chase.

All cats' eyes adapt quickly to low light or darkness. Their pupils enlarge and elongate to allow all the available light to enter. The incoming light is concentrated on the retina, the part of the eye that contains light-sensitive cells, or receptors. Behind the retina are other cells called tapetum lucidum. These cells act as reflectors. They direct light back through the retina to stimulate the receptors again, which greatly increases the animal's night vision. These reflector cells are what cause a cat's eyes to appear to shine in the dark.

With its sharp hearing, a cheetah is tuned-in to its environment. Unlike humans, a cheetah doesn't have to turn its head to hear the sounds around it. Its round outer ears move back and

Like all cats, cheetahs have excellent eyesight and hearing.

forth to funnel sound into the inner ear. The cheetah can then easily determine the direction from which the sound is coming and what is making it. Like all cats, cheetahs differ from other carnivores in the structure of their middle-ear cavities. A double layer of bone divides the auditory bulla. Scientists believe that this trait might increase a cat's sensitivity to sounds in its environment.

Because cheetahs rely primarily on vision when pursuing their prey, their sense of smell is less developed than it is in other animals. The sense of smell is important, however, for cheetahs to communicate with other cheetahs. Like many other animals, cheetahs have a sensory membrane called a vomeronasal organ, which is also known as Jacobson's organ. This pouchlike organ is located in the roof of the animal's mouth, right behind the incisors. It is lined with scent-detecting cells. In cats, the primary function of this organ relates to reproduction.

When a male cheetah smells a female's urine, he gets a strange expression on his face called a flehman grimace. He curls his lips, wrinkles his nose, opens his mouth, and raises his head. With these gestures, the animal draws in chemical molecules that are then picked up by the receptor cells of his Jacobson's organ. The female's scent lets the male know if she is ready to mate.

Whiskers, Toes, and Claws

Cat's whiskers are intriguing. These special hairs are extremely sensitive because their roots have nerve endings. Whiskers sprout from the face and other parts of the body. The long stiff mystical, or mustache, whiskers extend well beyond the jaws on both sides of the face. The shorter superciliary, or eyebrow, whiskers jut out from the skin above the eyes.

The cheetah's whiskers act as antennae. With them, the animal senses nearby obstacles that might injure its eyes, which is particularly helpful at night when vision is limited. The whiskers also help direct a cheetah to the most open path when hunting its prey—the less noise the cheetah makes, the closer it can get to the animal without scaring it away. The carpal hairs found on the back of the forelegs are also sensitive to touch.

Cats walk on their toes, not along the full length of their feet as humans do. They have five toes on their forefeet and four toes on their hind feet. There is no first toe—which would be in a position similar to a person's big toe—on the hind feet. The first toe of the forefoot is called a dewclaw. This toe is found on the back of the animal's leg and is always raised off the ground when the cat walks. The cheetah's dewclaws are hard, slightly curved, and sharp, forming deadly hooks. Scientists believe that cheetahs use them when fighting each other and when striking down a fleeing prey animal.

Cheetah Body

Each of the cheetah's toes sits on a soft pad. Each toe also ends in a claw that is blunt, like a dog's, and slightly curved. When a cheetah is at rest, the claws are retracted, or held off the ground. For a long time, people believed that the cheetah's claws did not retract as other cats' claws did. In fact, a cheetah's claws do partially retract but they do not have a sheath, or protective skin, to cover them. So, the tips of the claws are visible beyond the fur of the toes even when the claws are retracted.

Camouflage and Cooling

A cheetah's coat hangs loosely on the animal's body, as if it is too big. The coarse fur is short on the animal's back and legs but longer on the belly. The dense undercoat provides good insulation from the extremes of cold and hot temperatures. Long guard hairs, which carry dark spots, cover the undercoat. On some cheetahs, long hairs on the back of the neck form a short mane.

The cheetah's spotted coat provides camouflage and protection. The dark spots on the tawny fur background produces a pattern that makes it hard to see the animal in grass or brush. In the same way, the bold stripes of a tiger's fur or the spotted fur of a leopard blend into the patchy shade of woodlands and forests. When the cheetah is waiting for its prey, its coat hides it from view. The cheetah can then get close to the animal before beginning the chase.

All mammals regulate their body temperature to keep the temperature of the blood constant. When humans get hot, particularly after strenuous activity, their bodies cool by sweating. Cats also have sweat glands. These glands are located in their footpads, in the area under their tails, and in their skin. The glands in the skin are not for cooling but for protecting the skin from extremes of temperature. After a fast chase, when the cheetah gets overheated, it lowers its body temperature by panting. Panting forces extra air into the animal's mouth and nasal cavities, and its body cools down.

The cheetah's body is an incredible machine. Although it shares many physical characteristics with other cats, a cheetah's body is unique. It is the body of a champion runner and hunter. Until the twentieth century, African chiefs and rulers frequently wore a cheetah's skin—not only for its beauty but also as a symbol of authority and power.

FOLLOWING PAGES: THE LONG GRASSES ON THE PLAINS OF ZIMBABWE PROVIDE GOOD CAMOUFLAGE FOR CHEETAHS AS THEY WATCH FOR HERDS OF PREY.

4 Living Together

Many people know that the cheetah is a champion runner. Few people know much about the cat's social life, however, or its ability to communicate. Along with their great speed and unique hunting style, these characteristics set cheetahs apart from all the other cats.

Some cheetahs live alone, and others live in groups. They may live in groups for short periods of time or for their entire lives. Female cheetahs, like most wild cats, usually live alone unless they are caring for young. Females will gather with males for a day or longer to mate, and then leave again. Most male cheetahs do not live alone. Less than half of the males studied by biologist Tim Caro lived alone and remained independent throughout their lives.

ONCE SHE BECOMES A MOTHER, A FEMALE CHEETAH'S ONLY COMPANIONS ARE HER CUBS.

Male Coalitions

Most male cheetahs form groups, or coalitions, of two, three, or four members. Most often, the male cheetahs in a group were littermates. The coalitions exist for the lifetime of the cats. Occasionally, an unrelated male is accepted into the group, but often the outsider is driven away.

Why do male cheetahs live together, unlike other cats? What are the benefits of group living? These questions have provoked study, but scientists have not yet found any definite answers. One explanation proposed by Dr. Caro is that group living gives male cheetahs "the ability to control small territories and defend them against other males." They control territories that contain abundant prey and have optimal hunting conditions. These areas also attract many female cheetahs. As a result, male cheetahs living in coalitions have a greater opportunity to mate than do single males without territories.

Dr. Caro also found that males in coalitions ate more and spent more time eating. The males in a group could successfully hunt large prey animals, such as wildebeests. These large kills would provide all the members of the group with more meat. "Single males were thinner [than males living in groups] and often hungry," Dr. Caro found in his study of cheetahs in the Serengeti.

Companionship may also be a strong reason for group living. During the day, male cheetahs rest together and sleep close by each other. Grooming is an important daily ritual. They clean each other's face, ears, and neck with their raspy tongues. The act of grooming removes dirt, ticks, and flies from the animals' fur.

Group members make every effort to stay near each other. If, by chance, a male cheetah is separated from the others in his

CHEETAHS ALMOST SEEM TO FLY AS THEY RACE ACROSS THE OPEN GRASSLAND.

group, he becomes agitated. He searches and calls almost continuously as he tries to locate the other members of his coalition. Most male cheetah territories are small, so the animals are reunited within hours or within a day.

Sending Messages

Whether cheetahs live alone or in groups, they keep in touch with each other. They exchange information with scent, sound, and sight. Cheetahs scent-mark objects with their urine, feces, and secretions from special glands. Scent-marking by spraying with urine is the most effective method. Dr. Caro discovered that urine scent can last as long as three weeks.

As a male cheetah patrols its territory—the area it considers its own—the male checks for the scent of other cheetahs. The scent marks left on rocks, tree trunks, or other objects are chemical messages. They describe the owner's sex, identity, and, for a female, her readiness to mate. The patrolling cheetah sniffs the scent and then raises its head and opens its mouth—displaying the flehman grimace—to receive the messages. After about a minute, the cheetah may then raise its tail and squirt its own urine on top of the other animal's mark. The cheetah may also squat and rake the soil with its hind feet while urinating. Either way, the cheetah is sending outsiders the message that it owns that territory.

Cheetahs also leave feces covered by white mucus that is secreted from the glands under their tails. Unlike house cats or small wild cats, they don't bury the feces but rather leave it exposed on top of rocks, grass, or low termite mounds.

Additional scent glands are located on the cheetah's head and chin. Their sweat glands are between their toes. Sometimes, cheetahs lay down their scents by clawing at trees or fallen logs or by rubbing their heads and chins on grass or against hard surfaces. House cats exhibit the same marking behavior when they rub against furniture or their owners' legs.

When cheetahs meet, they may display several different types of behavior. Sometimes, a cheetah will see another cheetah

BACKING UP TO A TREE, A CHEETAH SPRAYS ITS SCENT ONTO THE TRUNK.

A PAIR OF CHEETAHS SNIFFS THE GROUND TO PICK UP THE SCENTS LEFT BY OTHER CHEETAHS.

off in the distance and simply turn and walk away. When they meet face-to-face, however, they communicate in several ways. They send distinct messages with their body postures, facial expressions, and vocal sounds.

When a cheetah is protecting its territory or kill from another cheetah, it stands with its back straight, its head held low, and its mouth open. The black tear mark on its face stands out. The hair on its neck and shoulders bristle. Its erect ears turn so that the backs of the ears face forward. The animal's tail thrashes wildly back and forth. Low growls, snarls, or hisses issue a warning. If these threats are successful, the intruder moves away.

When the cheetah is confronted by a stronger competitor, however—for example, a young animal facing a strong adult—the behavior changes. The less aggressive cheetah flattens its ears against the side of its head. The pupils of its eyes dilate, or widen. Its high-pitched yelps signal submission. The fearful cheetah may then squat down, roll onto its back exposing its belly, or just creep away. In these ways, the cheetah avoids the risk of a fight that could cause its injury or even death.

Cheetahs make a variety of vocal sounds. They make a short chirping sound that is similar to a birdcall. The chirp is made repeatedly at different volumes. Researchers doing field study have often been fooled—they look for the bird that is making the sound, only to see a cheetah come out of its hiding place. Cubs chirp when they are separated from their mothers or siblings.

A mother cheetah voices several types of calls to her cubs. The chirr, or churr, is a soft sound, which is often used with a chirp. Mothers call their cubs to follow with a churr or with prr-prr sounds. In case of danger, she may give a short high-pitched call to warn the cubs to remain motionless. A louder churring call, also called stutter barking, is a series of separate, throaty sounds. Males and some females stutter-bark before mating. After a kill, a cheetah protests angrily if a lion or hyena approaches to steal the prey. The cheetah growls, snarls, or hisses to scare the intruder. It may also moan with a loud *uuuu* sound as an added threat.

All cheetahs purr loudly when they are content. Continuous purring is commonly heard when cheetahs are resting together comfortably, when mothers are with their cubs, and when young animals are nursing. No one knows exactly how the cats

Sometimes the best defense against an intruder is a warning to move away.

make the purring sounds. Purring may occur when blood flow near the vocal cords increases. The sound gets louder as the cheetah breathes in and out.

Purring may also be related to the bony hyoid that cheetahs—and all other small cat species—have. The hyoid is a U-shaped bone in a cat's neck that supports the tongue and links the larynx, or voice box, to the skull. In the large cats, the hyoid is made partly of cartilage. The cartilage provides flexibility, which allows these large cats to roar. Cheetahs cannot roar, but the large cats—lions, tigers, leopards, jaguars, and snow leopards—cannot purr.

5 The Life Cycle

"WHEN THEY [THE CUBS] WERE YOUNG SHE
HAD ALWAYS SHOWN GREAT AFFECTION FOR
THEM, LICKING, AND NURSING THEM, AND
OFTEN SHE JOINED IN THEIR GAMES."

From *Pippa's Challenge*, Joy Adamson

Mating Behavior

By the time they are two years old, female cheetahs are ready to have their first litter of cubs. Males reach sexual maturity when they are two-and-a-half to three years old. Finding partners takes time, however, because many cheetahs travel alone across wide areas.

A female lets males know that she is ready to mate by scent marking—leaving her urine on rocks, tree trunks, or shrubs. The chemical messages in her scent tells any males nearby "I'm here and available." When a male "reads" her message, he will quickly

CHEETAH CUBS GROW FAST. BY THE TIME THEY ARE ABOUT THREE MONTHS OLD, THEY BEGIN TO LOOK LIKE ADULTS.

follow her trail. He does not know for certain if the female will accept him as her mate, however. So, he carefully approaches her, trying to get as close to her as possible to sniff her body or the area where she is sitting. He stutter-barks—a type of mating call. The female may stutter-bark, too, or she may respond by growling and slapping the male with her paw. If she does, he will slap her in return. Sometimes, the animals then groom themselves for a brief period, which helps to ease their nervousness. If the female decides to accept the male, she rolls on the ground, arches her back, and allows him to get close. It is not unusual, however, for the female to strike out at him again with her paw.

In typical cat behavior, while mating, the male cheetah grips the back of the female's neck and holds that position for a few seconds. The mating act lasts only a minute. Afterward, the male and female might separate right away, or they might stay together a day or two longer. After he has mated, the male's role is finished. He does not help the female raise their young.

With cheetahs that are bred in captivity, the story is slightly different. Female cheetahs in the breeding facilities do not need to seek their partners. Instead, potential mates are brought to them. "We focus on a particular female cheetah that we want to breed," says Susan Millard, an associate researcher at the San Diego Wild Animal Park in California. When the cheetah is in estrus, or sexual readiness, Millard introduces males into her pen. "Since I don't know who will respond to her and her to him, I test them every other day until I have a male that responds by stutter barking," she says. When the male makes that mating call, Millard knows the male will court the female and not attack her. "We allow plenty of time to find the right combination." According to Millard, female "cheetahs are still very selective when choosing their mates. Cheetahs are one of the more difficult felid species to get to reproduce. Their requirements and behavior are a bit more unique than other felids."

Baby Cheetahs

Wild cheetahs do not have a regular breeding season. Cheetah babies, called cubs, are born at any time of the year. The gestation period—the time during which the unborn cubs are carried in the mother's womb—is ninety-one to ninety-five days. During this period, the female remains within her territory. In the last days of her pregnancy, she finds an isolated place—a lair, or den—where she can give birth to her cubs. Often, it is hidden within a dense growth of shrubs, among boulders, or in tall grass. When choosing a lair, the female cheetah makes sure that there is a source of food nearby.

A female cheetah may give birth to as many as eight cubs, but the average number is three or four. The newborn cubs are tiny. They weigh from eight to eleven ounces (250 to 300 grams)—less than a pound! Their eyes, which are closed at birth, open about eleven days later. Long, blue-gray fur cloaks the upper parts of their bodies. Their small bellies, tails, and legs are covered with solid, dark spots. This distinctive coloring disappears after the cubs are three months old. The colors probably help to camouflage the very young cubs, hiding them from predators like lions, leopards, and hyenas. A female that fears for the safety of her litter will move them to a new den. She carries each cub separately, grasping the skin on the back of its neck in her mouth. The female also changes lairs every few days to control the buildup of odors that might attract enemies and biting flies.

For the first six to eight weeks, cheetah cubs rely on their

CHEETAH CUBS STAY CLOSE TO THEIR MOTHER FOR PROTECTION AGAINST LIONS AND HYENAS.

mother's rich milk for food. She stays with them, keeping them warm and clean, and allowing them to nurse for as long as eight hours or more. The young cubs grow rapidly. After ten days, they can crawl and, after three weeks, they can walk steadily. As the cubs grow and need more food, the female starts to leave the den to hunt for meat. Her comings and goings from the den are dangerous because they may draw the attention of predators. The mother cheetah stays alert, however, and waits and watches before reentering the den where her cubs are hidden. While their mother is away hunting, the cubs stay inside, nestled together to keep warm.

Cheetah cubs are extremely playful. They chase and wrestle each other. They stalk and pounce from hiding places as if practicing their hunting skills. They slap each other with their paws to send one another tumbling. In *Pippa's Challenge*, a book about a female cheetah's life, author Joy Adamson wrote that she had watched cubs playing "king of the hill" on a pile of gravel. "Then they amused themselves with hide and seek and often their mother joined the game."

By the time cheetah cubs are two months old, they are strong, agile, and better coordinated. They are ready to leave the den and follow their mother on the hunt. At first, she leaves her young cubs waiting in the grass while she hunts. Very young cubs sometimes whimper or chirp when separated from their mothers for the first time. Their cries may alert the prey to the mother cheetah's presence and cause her hunt to fail. When the mother cheetah succeeds in catching her prey, she calls to the cubs to join her and encourages them to eat. Often, the prey animal is small and the cubs are nearby, so the mother drags the dead animal to them.

The cubs are cautious at first because the carcass is a strange object to them. They watch their mother to learn what to do.

Cheetah cubs are very playful. They play-fight and chase each other while they grow stronger and more coordinated.

Gradually, they lose their fear and begin to eat. They need their mother's help to cut through the prey's tough hide. She opens up the animal's body where the skin is soft and there are no bones. The young cubs' teeth and jaws are small and not yet well developed. For them, chewing the meat is a slow process. It might take the family more than an hour to finish their meal. They leave behind only the prey animal's head and thick leg bones.

After sharing their meal, the cheetah family finds a shady spot to rest. They clean each other's faces and fur with their tongues. Contented, they lie close together, purring loudly before dozing off for a midday nap.

The cubs continue to feed on their mother's milk until they

are about four months old. After that, they only eat the meat that their mother provides or that they hunt themselves. At eight months of age, the cubs lose their baby teeth and grow larger and stronger permanent teeth.

At times, a cheetah cub may get separated from its mother, or the mother dies. With luck, orphans can survive by connecting with another family and stealing bits of food from them. The new family usually allows the cub to join them—although the new mother may not be welcoming at first. She keeps the orphan on the fringe of her family's life by hissing and making other warnings. An adopted cheetah may stay with the new family for a few days or months—or until it becomes a good hunter.

Learning to Hunt

The first months of life are critical for cheetah cubs. According to Dr. Tim Caro, less than one-third of the cubs born in the Serengeti National Park in East Africa live to leave their dens. Scientists estimate that only five out of every one hundred cheetah cubs born in East Africa survive to adulthood.

Young cubs are defenseless. They cannot move around very well, which makes them vulnerable to attack by lions and hyenas. Small cubs sometimes perish in grass fires and from exposure during heavy rains. Parasites and insect pests also weaken the health of young cubs. Occasionally, a mother will abandon her litter if prey is scarce in that area.

When they first leave their den for the open plains, the young cubs are afraid of every creature they meet. They show their fear by hissing and running away, even if the animals are harmless giraffes or birds. Their mother remains watchful for real dangers. If she detects a predator in the distance, she moves her cubs to safety. If the danger is close by, she threatens the predator by growling and hissing, and, sometimes, by attacking it. While she is chasing the animal away, the cubs have a chance to run and hide. Often, however, the mother cannot distract or chase off the predator. The attacking animal may then chase and kill the youngest cubs. The older cheetah cubs can outrun a lion or leopard.

As the cubs grow older, they become more aware of their surroundings and the predators around them. Following their mother's example, they glance up often while eating and keep watch even when resting. Like other carnivores, cheetah cubs also develop basic hunting skills in the first year of life. Gaining those skills is a slow, gradual process. The young cheetahs must learn and practice for a long time before they become skillful hunters.

First, the cubs must learn how to recognize and select the prey animal. They must also learn how to stalk their prey without being seen. Through trial and error, the cubs learn to judge distance and the right time to begin the chase. Finally, they learn how to knock down their prey and kill it.

Cheetahs hunt in the daytime—either in early morning or late afternoon. At first, young cubs watch their mother from a distance or play in the grass, waiting for her to return or call to them to eat. When they are three months old, the cubs are stronger and able to travel with their mother throughout her large home range. They walk, trot, or run after all types of prey. These young cubs chase birds or small carnivores, such as black-backed jackals and bat-eared foxes. They do not usually catch their prey—but they are gaining valuable hunting experience.

When the cubs are three to four months old, their mother brings them a live animal—a newborn gazelle, perhaps, or a small hare. She releases the animal so that the cubs can catch and kill it. She does not show the cubs what to do. Instead, she

IN THE MASAI MARA NATIONAL RESERVE, THIS MOTIONLESS YOUNG CUB PRACTICES STALKING.

relies on their natural instincts to teach them. At first, the cubs are clumsy. If the prey animal escapes, the mother cheetah catches it and brings it back again to continue the lesson. She allows the cubs a short time to practice their skills, then she kills the prey animal herself.

Only cheetah cubs six months or older are strong enough to suffocate small prey themselves. By that time, the cubs begin to lead the family hunts. Their mother still hunts with them, and she is usually the one that captures the family's meal. The female cheetah may also catch a prey animal and then release the animal so that the cubs can chase it and kill it.

When the cubs are ten months old, their mother gives them more opportunities to hunt by themselves. Usually, the young

A FAWN IS THE CENTER OF ATTENTION FOR TWO ADOLESCENT CHEETAHS.

cubs do not succeed, however. Hunting takes patience and timing. These young cheetahs often don't stay hidden, and the prey animals notice them and run off. Cubs also often start the chase too early or from too far away, which also gives the hunted animal a chance to flee. Even if the cubs do catch up with their prey, they may lack the confidence to knock it down and kill it.

Cheetah cubs stay close to their mothers and rely on her for food until they are fourteen to eighteen months old. By then, they are nearly grown. Gradually, they separate from her. Brothers and sisters remain together for several more months. The mother may have already become pregnant with her next litter. In some cases, the mother does not become pregnant again until after the cubs leave.

Adulthood

Adolescent cheetah cubs are hunters in training—and being hungry is the best teacher. Thomson's gazelles head the list of the cheetah's favorite prey species. Single, female cheetahs hunt newborn gazelles and gazelle fawns because they are the easiest to snare. Sibling cheetahs hunting together catch adult gazelles. With practice and experience, a cheetah's hunting abilities improve greatly as the animal grows and matures.

Male littermates continue to live together, either for several years or for their entire lives. While they are still young, the brothers may even allow an unrelated male to join their group. The young adult males then move away from their mother's home range.

A young female cheetah separates from her littermates when she is two years old. She establishes her own home range—which overlaps the familiar environs of her mother's home range. If the mother and daughter happen to meet on the shared territory, they simply walk away. Within a few months of separation from her mother and siblings, the young female is ready to mate and have a first litter of her own.

Because cheetahs roam widely, it is difficult to judge exactly how long they live in the wild. Males probably live about eight to eleven years. Males that live in permanent territories live longer than individual males that wander. Female cheetahs have the tough job of raising their cubs and have a shorter life span of six to eight years. Captive cheetahs in zoos and other facilities may live for twelve to seventeen years.

6 At Home and On the Move

When a female cheetah is not caring for her cubs, she lives alone. She travels and hunts in a large area called a home range. Within this area, she has a plentiful supply of prey animals for food. The trees and shrubs provide her with many hiding places and shady areas. In his studies, biologist Tim Caro found that some cheetah home ranges in the Serengeti are as large as 508 square miles (1,269 sq km). Other, smaller ranges are about one-fifth that size. The average size of a cheetah home range is 333 square miles (833 sq km)—that's seven times the area of the city of San Francisco, California!

In a year, a female cheetah travels throughout her entire home range, following the migratory herds of Thomson's gazelles. When the gazelles move, the cheetah must move with them if she is going to eat. She stays with them in each location for weeks at a time. In general, a female with cubs may travel about two-and-a-half miles (4 km) in a day. Dr. Tim Caro observed "one

RESTING TOGETHER IN THE SHADE, THIS FAMILY GROUP FINDS RELIEF FROM THE MIDDAY HEAT.

mother with four recently emerged two-month-old cubs covering seven miles [11 km] in a twelve-and-a-half-hour stretch." How remarkable for such small cubs to endure such a long trek! A female's home range may overlap other cheetah ranges—including her own mother's—but she does not fight to defend it against either males or other females.

Residents

Some male cheetahs also live alone. Others may belong to a group of two or more males, called a coalition. Sometimes, a single male cheetah will establish a territory. More often, coalitions establish territories. The cheetahs actively patrol and defend these well-marked areas. On the Serengeti grasslands, a territory may cover fifteen to thirty square miles (39 to 78 sq km). These territorial males, called residents, form territories in areas where there is good landscape cover. Cover refers to the large shrubs, thick mounds of grass, rocky outcrops, or low depressions that provide hiding places and shade. Often, female cheetahs travel into male territories that have ample prey and cover. The males then have more frequent opportunities to mate.

Resident cheetahs outline the borders of their territory by spraying urine, depositing feces, or leaving claw marks. These scent marks are clearly visible on large rocks, tree trunks, or protruding termite hills. After frequent scent-marking, the residents have clearly identified the territory as theirs. Their scent marks warn all other males passing through that the area is inhabited: Keep out, or you risk a fight! The competition for male territory is intense and constant. The ownership of a territory may change suddenly or may last for a year or more. A single resident male is less able to hold and defend his territory for a long time. He may be chased out by a coalition after only a few months. A coalition may lose its territory by being forced out or killed by younger, stronger males. There is strength in numbers, however—a three-member coalition can sometimes hold onto a territory for a year or longer. In some cases, a territory may simply be abandoned when one member of the resident group dies or disappears. The remaining male knows that he cannot control the territory alone and so he leaves it.

Resident males do not usually wander outside of their territories unless prey becomes scarce. Then, they will travel to a neighboring area to hunt for several days or a few weeks before returning to their own home base.

Nomads

Males without territories are called nomads, or floaters. They can be any age—from adolescents and young adults to elderly males. Nomads roam from one area to another. They are shadowy figures. They try to remain hidden from predators and from other male cheetahs. They often travel at night and hide in tall grasses during the day. In both the Serengeti and Namibia, a nomad's home range may average three hundred square miles (780 sq km)—which is ten to twenty times larger than a resident male's territory. Frequently, the home ranges overlap one another as the nomadic males follow traveling females and gazelles. When an adult nomad spots a female, he attempts to approach her. He tries to get close enough to detect signs that she is in estrus, or ready to mate. If she is not yet ready, he may wait several days.

Although they have no need to scent-mark territory, nomads sometimes do scent-mark while they are traveling through other males' territory. The nomad runs the risk of serious injury or death, however. The residents sometimes try to drive the intruder away with warnings. If that doesn't work, they attack viciously. It is impossible for one male cheetah to defend himself against two or more males. The animals will bite deeply again and again, pulling out great chunks of fur and flesh. If the injured male cannot escape, the residents will kill him with a bite to the throat.

Hunting for Food

Cheetahs are diurnal, which means that they are active during the daytime, when other predators sleep. These big cats rely on their eyesight to locate prey, and they either hunt in the early morning or late in the afternoon. Often, they climb to a high place to scan the area for prey and for enemies. Cheetahs in Namibia run up the sloping trunks and large horizontal branches of trees to view the landscape. These trees are called play trees, and they are an important part of a cheetah's life. Cheetahs routinely move from one play tree to another within their territories.

Most cats try to get as close as possible to their prey before pouncing to catch it. Cheetahs, however, rely on their great speed to catch their prey. They use different hunting methods, depending upon the season, the landscape, and the behavior of the prey animals. Generally, a cheetah stalks its prey. It hides under the cover of grass clumps, bushes, or low areas while moving steadily and slowly closer to the herd. When the cheetah is about seventy yards (63 m) away, the cat abruptly gallops toward the herd, and the animals flee. The cheetah selects one victim and, in a burst of power, accelerates to full speed. The chase covers about 550 yards (500 m) and may be over in just twenty seconds. As the cheetah catches up to its quarry, it either trips the fleeing animal or knocks it off balance with a swat to its hind legs. Once the animal is on the ground, the cheetah grabs the victim's throat in its jaws. In four to five minutes, the captured prey stops breathing. It takes the

CHEETAHS HUNT ALMOST ENTIRELY BY SIGHT. ADOLESCENT CHEETAHS, SHOWING THE SHORT MANE ON THE BACK OF THEIR NECKS, SCAN THE SURROUNDINGS FOR PREY OR WATCH FOR ENEMIES.

cheetah another fifteen to twenty minutes to catch its breath.

Rather than trying to surprise their prey, coalition males often walk directly toward a herd of gazelles In this case, it is not unusual for the antelopes to run off. Sometimes, the antelopes just stand and watch the cheetahs approach. Without the element of

HOLDING AN ANTELOPE BY THE THROAT, THE CHEETAH SUFFOCATES ITS PREY.

surprise, however, these cheetahs are less successful in the hunt. On some occasions, a cheetah gets lucky—and a herd of gazelles moves in its direction. The cheetah then just sits or squats and waits for the herd to get closer before giving chase. Other times, the prey animals are so absorbed in grazing that they fail to notice the predators nearby. In these situations, the cheetah again has the advantage and may start its pursuit sooner than it usually would.

One of the most favorable times for cheetahs to hunt is just after large numbers of gazelles have been born—which occurs within a period of a few weeks. The mothers lay the helpless newborns in clumps of grass or bushes to keep them safe from predators. The fawns will stay hidden until they are strong enough to travel with the herd. For cheetahs, these days are a time of plenty. They nose through the grass and search for the hidden young. The fawns—and occasional small hares—are easily overtaken and caught by the big cats. Cheetahs strangle the gazelles to kill them, but bite through the skulls of smaller animals like hares. On rare occasions, a mother gazelle or wildebeest will try to rescue its fawn from a cheetah's jaws. Fighting with its sharp horns and hooves, the mother might be able to save the young animal. If there are two or more cheetahs attacking, however, one will distract the mother while the other grabs the calf.

Hunting takes skill and experience, but conditions must also be just right for success. Even experienced cheetahs fail. Hunts usually fail because the prey animals spot the approaching cheetahs and run off. The cheetahs might also try to tackle a large adult animal, such as a wildebeest or a Grant's gazelle, but be unable to bring it down. Females with cubs are only successful about one-third of the time when pursuing adult Thomson's gazelles. Single or paired males fare no better. Coalitions of three or more males catch their kill about half of the time.

After a cheetah has killed its prey, it drags the animal's carcass to a safe place. After it catches its breath the cheetah eats all the meat—leaving only the animal's skin, bones, and entrails, or intestines. The size of the prey and the number of "diners at the table" determine how often cheetahs need to hunt. An adult Thomson's gazelle, which weighs an average of about forty-four pounds (20 kg), will feed a mother and her medium-sized cubs for one day. A small fawn will leave the cheetah family hungry for more.

SPECIES OF ANIMALS HUNTED BY CHEETAHS

In East Africa:
Thomson's gazelle
Grant's gazelle
Savanna hare
Impala
Springbok
Dik-dik
Steinbok
Wildebeest
Topi
Reedbuck
Eland
Kori bustard

In Namibia:
Springbok
Greater kudu
Black-faced impala
Blue wildebeest

In Botswana:
Springbok
Steinbok
Lechwe
Blue wildebeest
Common reedbuck

Greater kudu, Hwange, Zimbabwe

Blue wildebeest, Etosha National Park, Namibia

Springbok,
Etosha
National
Park,
Namibia

Black-faced impala, Etosha National Park, Namibia

On the Serengeti plains in Eastern Africa, Thomson's gazelles are the prey of choice for cheetahs. A single male cheetah kills about seventy-eight adult gazelles in a year. Females with young cubs kill about sixty a year. Even adolescents snare their fair share. Coalitions of two or more cheetahs don't kill as many Thomson's gazelles. These male groups prefer larger animals, such as Grant's gazelles, wildebeests, and topis (a type of antelope). These animals provide the cheetahs with more meat and can easily satisfy the hunger of the entire group.

The type of prey varies in different areas of Africa. In northern Namibia, cheetahs hunt adult and young springbok (a type of gazelle), kudu and black-faced impala (types of antelope), blue wildebeests, and other animals. In the dry grassland of southern Botswana, cheetahs find springbok, blue wildebeests, and various types of antelope, such as steenbok, lechwe, and common reedbuck. When their favorite prey is scarce, cheetahs eat whatever they can catch: ostriches and other birds, warthogs, lizards, frogs, hares, and eggs.

Cheetahs need water as well as food. The meat and blood of the animals they eat give the cheetahs some liquid, so the animals only need to visit a watering hole every four or five days. If the weather conditions are extremely hot and dry, as in semidesert habitats, the cheetahs will eat the juicy tsama melon—a "water bag" inside a rind.

Disease and Other Threats

Cheetahs, like all animals, sometimes get sick. Scientists believe that cheetahs have a low resistance to disease because of inbreeding—mating only within a small group of related individuals. After a long period of inbreeding, the genes of a species may be very similar. The species is then said to lack "genetic

THE WILDEBEEST TURNS SHARPLY AS IT TRIES TO EVADE THE PURSUING CHEETAH.

diversity." Genetic diversity helps the species fight disease. Viruses, bacteria, and parasites can threaten the entire cheetah population of a region.

A cheetah that is under stress from injuries or lack of food will show signs of poor health. The animal may lose weight. Its coat may be coarse and covered with mange, a skin disease that is caused by tiny mites. The cheetah's sores or wounds may ooze, and its mouth may be painfully infected. Wild cheetahs in this type of condition are not likely to live long.

 Even healthy cheetahs are troubled by internal and external parasites. Parasites are small organisms that live on or in another organism, which is called the host organism. Parasites get their food and protection from their host. External parasites, like ticks, mites, and fleas, attack a cheetah most often in the areas around the ears, neck, and rump. Their blood-sucking bites irritate the animal's skin and sometimes transmit disease.

Internal parasites, or worms, are common among wild cheetahs, too. Flatworms, round worms, and tapeworms live in the animal's intestines. A healthy animal can survive without ill effects. An already-hungry cheetah, however, may become weaker because of the parasites. The animal would then be more vulnerable to diseases caused by bacteria and viruses. The bacterial disease of tuberculosis can cause death. Viruses—such as cat distemper or feline infectious gastroenteritis—spread quickly and easily from animal to animal. Cheetahs are also prone to a viral disease called feline infectious peritonitis (FIP). This disease causes the lining of the abdomen to become inflamed. In captivity, where cheetahs are living close to each other and other cats, feline viral diseases spread quickly. Wild cheetahs have a lower risk of viral disease. They live in dry areas, eat fresh meat, and do not eat carrion, or rotting flesh, which may carry disease, like lions and other big cats do. Also, because cheetahs live at a distance from each other, there is less chance of the spread of disease.

Disease can be devastating to a cheetah population, but it just one of the constant threats that cheetahs face. Cheetahs are the least aggressive of the large cats. This trait makes life more difficult for them. Predators, particularly lions and hyenas, steal their food—sometimes, before the cheetah has a chance to eat at all. These carnivores, including the powerful leopard, frequently kill cheetah cubs. When given the opportunity, these cats will attack adult cheetahs, too, often wounding or killing them. Territorial fights between male cheetahs also result in many deaths or injuries. But the biggest threat to the survival of cheetahs is the people who destroy their habitats.

7 The Race for Survival

Thousands of years ago, cheetahs ranged widely throughout the semiarid lands of Africa, across Arabia and Asia Minor, and as far east as India. Rulers of the ancient kingdoms—pharaohs, kings, and, later, Mogul princes—kept the sleek cats as pets and relied on their speed during royal hunting trips.

By the middle of the twentieth century, however, cheetahs were extinct in India. In Africa, their ranges and numbers had shrunk. In 1970, one survey estimated that there were between 7,000 and 23,000 cheetahs in the world, widely scattered in

THE FUTURE OF THESE FAST, FIERCE PREDATORS IS VERY UNCERTAIN. THE LARGE TRACTS OF LAND CHEETAHS NEED FOR HUNTING HAVE BEEN SHRINKING FOR MANY YEARS.

Africa with a small number in Iran. Today, the number of cheetahs has dropped to approximately ten thousand. About one thousand are scattered through northern, western, and central Africa, but the majority are in East Africa (3,000), Namibia (2,500 to 3,000), Botswana (1,000 to 2,000), and Zimbabwe (500 to 1,000).

How did this happen? Why is one of the most beautiful cats in the world endangered, or threatened with becoming extinct? There are many reasons, but the loss of natural habitat tops the list. Cheetahs need large tracts of grassland with a plentiful supply of antelopes to hunt. Today, throughout Africa, farms are taking over areas that were once open to cheetahs. Because of growing populations, towns are springing up, and new roads crisscross what were once wild lands. Both the predators and the prey species are affected by the loss of their natural habitat. There is less land for cheetahs to live on, and fewer prey animals for them to hunt. Even in the best conditions, a cheetah's life is difficult as it competes with other carnivores for food and space.

The conflicts between animals and people are increasing, too. Farmers and ranchers kill cheetahs because they are afraid that the animals will destroy their livestock. Growing numbers of people who trap and shoot cheetahs threaten their survival. With more guns and all-terrain vehicles available, hunting for cheetahs has become easier—although it is against the law in twenty-four African countries. Only Namibia, Zambia, and Zimbabwe permit trophy hunting. Illegal poaching also continues in many places. Poachers sell the cheetah skins, which are made into expensive fur coats, pillows, and wall decorations.

The Story of Namibia

In Namibia, on the southwestern coast of Africa, three-quarters of the wildlife and almost all of the cheetahs are free-ranging—the animals live on private lands, not in protected reserves. Throughout the 1950s, Namibian farmers reduced the number of wild grazing animals that competed with their livestock for grass. They also killed the lions and hyenas that preyed on their cattle and sheep. Without these natural enemies harassing them, the number of cheetahs grew rapidly. Cheetahs, leopards, caracal, and black-backed jackals became the main predators in Namibia.

In the early 1980s, the grassland suffered from a serious drought that hit the country. Ranchers destroyed more of the wild grazing animals, to save the sparse grass for their cattle. In addition, the deadly viral disease of rabies swept through herds of kudu, one of the cheetah's favorite species of prey. Because they did not have enough prey animals to eat, the hungry cheetahs went after sheep, goats, and calves. Ranchers estimated that cheetahs took more than ten percent of their calves. They declared an all-out war on the cats. Between 1980 and 1991, about seven thousand cheetahs—one-half of the total population—were killed. Of those, nearly 6,000 were shot. The rest were trapped alive and sent out of the country. To most Namibian farmers and ranchers, cheetahs are pests that should be shot—or trapped first and then shot.

Habitat loss continues in Namibia as brush (shrubs and trees) replaces the grasslands. The drought set the stage, but ranching practices have brought great changes to the landscape. Too many head of cattle have grazed on the grasslands, stripping them bare and causing the soil to erode. The natural fires that burn brush and rejuvenate the grasses were controlled. With the loss of the large browsing animals, such as rhinos and elephants, the brush took over the grasses. Browsers eat young, bushy plants to keep the brush from invading grasslands.

CHEETAHS SEEM PERPLEXED BY A WARNING FOR TOURISTS ABOUT CHEETAHS. IN FACT, THE TABLES HAVE TURNED. CHEETAHS ARE AT RISK DUE TO PEOPLE.

Something had to be done about the situation. In 1989, Dieter Morsbach, a researcher for the South West Africa Department of Nature Conservation, began gathering facts about the causes of conflict between farmers and cheetahs. Soon, he learned that the farmers and ranchers held the key to the survival of cheetahs in Namibia. In 1991, Laurie Marker, who had previously worked with the cheetah-breeding program in Oregon, moved to Namibia. There, she founded the nonprofit Cheetah Conservation Fund (CCF). Its aim is to protect free-ranging cheetahs by providing them with safe habitats.

Laurie, with her pet cheetah at her side, talks to any farmer who will listen. She discusses ways to reduce their livestock losses. She encourages farmers to corral young calves to protect them from predators. Keeping donkeys in the animals' pen also provides extra security for the calves. Donkeys have a natural dislike for dogs, jackals, and cheetahs, and they will chase the animals away. Farmers can also rely on large guard dogs. Dogs have been used for centuries to defend flocks of the sheep and goats. These simple steps have helped to decrease farmers' losses of livestock and protect cheetahs from destruction.

Some farmers still trap cheetahs by placing wire box traps near the cheetah's play tree. The trapped animal used to be killed on the spot. Today, the farmer may call the CCF or AfriCat, another conservation group. These groups remove the cheetahs from the traps and release them into a game reserve. CCF and AfriCat have reluctantly supported trophy hunting—the killing of cheetahs for sport. The group believes that this type of hunting will at least encourage farmers to allow cheetahs to live on their land. Hunting parties pay for the right to hunt game on the farmer's property. For every animal shot, the hunter pays the

TOURISTS IN MINIVANS FOLLOW THIS CHEETAH. VANS MAY DISTRACT CHEETAHS FROM HUNTING SUCCESSFULLY.

farmer a trophy fee. Because of these practices, some farmers' attitudes toward wild cheetahs have turned around. The trophy fee gives them a monetary inducement not to shoot or trap the cats themselves.

The CCF is located in Otjiwarongo, Namibia, within three

adjoining farms that total 38,000 acres (15,200 hectares). A recent donation added another 10,000 acres (4,000 ha), which will be used as a research station for scientists and students. An important part of CCF's work is education and research. Ranchers, students, and local villagers travel to its education center to learn about the cheetah's role in the environment. Ranchers are also encouraged to form groups to promote ecologically friendly ranching practices. The organization's researchers work with the cheetahs themselves. They place tags and radio collars on the animals so that they can keep track of them and learn more about their home ranges, territories, and numbers. Researchers are also working to identify the type of farm ecosystem that will best support cheetahs and other wild animals.

AfriCat is a nonprofit group based in central Namibia. It was founded by Wayne and Lise Hanssen in November 1992 to protect cheetahs and other cats from farmers. AfriCat has rescued more than two hundred cheetahs and one hundred leopards from traps. If the predators have not killed livestock, they are released or relocated elsewhere. Animals that have preyed on livestock are given a new home in a game reserve. Like CCF, AfriCat also educates farmers about ways to prevent loss of livestock. They have installed electric fencing on a number of farms to prevent predators from entering. Schoolchildren visit AfriCat's farm to learn about the role of cheetahs and other big cats in the environment. These children—many of whom may be future farmers—have the chance to meet a cheetah face-to-face.

Parks and Reserves

Although most of Africa's cheetahs are free-ranging as in Namibia, a small number live in national parks and reserves. About five to six hundred cheetahs inhabit the vast Serengeti

EACH CHEETAH HAS A UNIQUE PATTERN OF SPOTS ON ITS CHEST, LEGS, AND TAIL THAT HELPS RESEARCHERS IDENTIFY INDIVIDUALS.

National Park in Tanzania. There, the only threats to cheetahs are from natural predators, fights among themselves, diseases, and, possibly, weakness from inbreeding.

Wherever cheetahs coexist with their predators—lions, hyenas, and leopards—the size of the population is affected. In the Serengeti, for example, only five out of one hundred cheetah cubs live to become independent. Lions and hyenas seek out the helpless cubs and kill them. The death of so many cubs may be one reason for the low cheetah population in the park.

Cheetahs that live in small, confined areas—like a park and reserve—are more likely to be threatened by illness, too. These animals have fewer choices when mating. As they continue to breed with related animals, the species becomes weaker. They almost become carbon copies of one another. This lack of genetic diversity makes the animals more prone to disease. Because the animals live so close together, when one cheetah becomes ill from a virus, there is a good chance that the virus will spread throughout the entire population. Inbreeding also results in more stillbirths (death at birth), premature births, and the poor health of young cubs.

A Secure Future

Does the future for cheetahs lie in zoos? Captive-breeding programs offer hope that the species will not become extinct. Yet, in the past, cheetahs in captivity have not bred successfully. Many people thought that this was because the male's sperm had been reduced or damaged through inbreeding. Because the captive cheetahs did not reproduce, zoos filled their cages with wild cheetahs.

The first cheetah birth in a zoo occurred at the Philadelphia

Zoo in 1956. The three cubs died shortly after birth but the unusual event created great excitement. Zoo keepers were encouraged to continue trying to solve the riddle of breeding cheetahs in captivity. First, however, they needed animals to breed. Hundreds of cheetahs were exported from southwestern Africa to zoos and wild animal parks everywhere. An early successful breeding attempt that was successful took place at Whipsnade Zoo in England. The keepers at this zoo worked with the natural behavior of the animals. Females lived apart from the males until they were ready to mate—just as they do in the wild. The females were also given a safe place to raise their young, and the cubs survived to raise young of their own. Other successes followed. The De Wildt Cheetah and Wildlife Centre in South Africa has produced more than five hundred cheetah cubs since 1971. Whenever possible, the animals are reintroduced into the wild or sent to other captive-breeding centers. De Wildt was also the first breeder of the rare king cheetah.

In the past twenty years, more than one hundred cubs have been born at both the San Diego Wild Animal Park and the Wildlife Safari in Oregon. They and other North American zoos are working together to carefully manage a healthy breeding population. This work is made possible by the Species Survival Plan and its committee of scientists. The age, parents, offspring, health, and previous homes of each cheetah are listed in a stud book or computer file. The zoos cooperate with each other and transfer animals as needed to ensure genetic diversity. The foremost goal in this program is to ensure the stability of the species.

According to Susan Millard, the San Diego Wild Animal Park has features "that are unique and certainly contribute to our breeding success. We have a lot of space so we can move the animals from place to place and put them in different enclosures.

THE CHEETAH IS AN ELEGANT CAT WITH LONG LEGS, A SLENDER BODY, AND A BEAUTIFUL SPOTTED COAT. IF ENOUGH PEOPLE TAKE AN INTEREST IN THESE MAGNIFICENT CATS, SURELY WE CAN IMPROVE THEIR CHANCE OF SURVIVAL IN THE YEARS TO COME.

Just moving to a new area can stimulate these animals. We change pens, give them new neighbors, new things to see." New mothers have the use of a birthing house with a heated floor. A video camera records the activities within the house to be sure the cubs are thriving. Cleanliness and a balanced diet are also vital to the cheetahs' health. They receive a beef-based meal with added vitamins and minerals. Occasionally, they get some bones or a chicken for a change of pace.

The success of captive-breeding programs will ensure the cheetah's place in zoological parks. Although there are no plans to reintroduce captive-bred cheetahs into the wild, their presence there is also important to the preservation of the species. Efforts to save the cheetah also include finding ways to preserve and protect their natural habitats and programs to educate young and old about the important role that these animals play in our natural world. As scientists continue to learn more about these cats and their behavior, we may discover new ways to preserve and protect these champions of the animal world.

Cheetahs are survivors. For thousands of years, they have endured predators, disease, and environmental challenges— and they have continued to live. Although these powerful cats have proven their great, natural ability to take care of themselves, their future lies in our hands.

Glossary

adapt—change or develop in ways that aid survival in the environment

captivity—the state of being held captive

carcass—the dead body of an animal

carnivore—a meat-eating animal

coursing—a hunting practice in which trained animals help hunters pursue their game

cubs—the young of certain mammals, such as cheetahs, lions, wolves, and bears

evolution—process by which species, or types of plants and animals, change over time, with new species emerging from old ones

felid—cat

habitat—natural environment in which a plant or animal lives and grows

inbreeding—mating that takes place only within a small group of related individuals

litter—all the babies that are born to a female mammal at one time

mammal—animal with backbone that nourishes its young with milk from the mother's mammary glands

mutation—a genetic change in an animal that is passed on to its young

natural selection—process of evolution that takes place over a very long period of time to ensure that the strongest qualities of a species survive

nomad—a person or animal that roams from place to place rather than living in a permanent settlement

predator—an animal that preys upon other living creatures for food

prey—the animal that a carnivore hunts, kills, and eats for food

savanna—an open grassland with scattered trees

ungulates—hoofed mammals, such as gazelles and other types of antelope, which are usually also herbivores, or plant-eating animals

wildebeest—a large African antelope with curved horns

Species Checklist

Plants and animals have both common and scientific names. Common names are written in lower case, unless the name is taken from a proper noun. Scientific names, which are in Latin, should be italicized, with the first, or generic, name capitalized and the following names, which identify the species and subspecies, in lowercase.

There is only one species of cheetah, and its scientific name is *Acinonyx jubatus*. The five subspecies are listed below, along with some key facts.

Acinonyx jubatus jubatus
range: South Africa
characteristics: small body size; small, well-separated spots on coat

Acinonyx jubatus raineyii
range: East Africa, west and east of the Kikuya fault characteristics: generally paler and longer
hair than *Acinonyx jubatus*, especially on the belly and back of neck; large spots close
together; some animals have fewer spots on the back

Acinonyx jubatus soemmeringii
range: Sudan
characteristics: pale hair; small spots widely separated; hind feet spotted

Acinonyx jubatus hecki
range: Northwest Africa
characteristics: small body size, dainty; pale hair

Acinonyx jubatus venaticus
former range: India and North Africa
characteristics: smaller than East African cheetahs, with shorter legs; no long hair on back of
neck and belly; small spots widely spaced like those of *Acinonyx jubatus jubatus*

Further Research

The books listed here are just a small number of the books about cheetahs that are available in libraries and bookstores. A selection of interesting and informative Web sites is also included.

Books for Young People

MacMillan, Dianne. *Cheetahs*. Minneapolis, MN: Carolrhoda Books, 1997.

Morrison, Taylor. *Cheetah*. New York: Henry Holt & Co., 1998.

Zoobooks. *Cheetahs*. Poway, CA: Wildlife Education, 2000.

Web Sites

www.african-edventure.org leads visitors on a virtual trek across Africa. Through an online diary, photographs, videos, e-mails, a discussion board, and maps, visitors can participate in this African Edventure from home.

www.africat.org is the web site of AfriCat, a nonprofit organization based in Namibia, Africa. AfriCat is dedicated to the protection of wild cats in farming communities. The site contains pages about the cheetahs and leopards of Africa and the many efforts being made to protect them. AfriCat also sponsors an adopt-a-cheetah program.

www.aza.org is the web site of the American Zoo and Aquarium Association. The site features photographs and facts sheets about cheetahs and other big cats. It also provides a listing of zoos and aquariums by state.

www.cheetah.org is the web site of the Cheetah Conservation Fund in Namibia, Africa. The organization was started in 1991 by Laurie Marker to provide safe habitats for free-ranging cheetahs. The site contains a biography of founder Laurie Marker, a Kids Page, and links to many other sites about cheetahs.

www.dewildt.org.za is the web site of the De Wildt Cheetah and Wildlife Centre in South Africa. The site contains information about efforts to breed cheetahs in captivity, a photo gallery, and an on-line tour of the habitats of several wild animals.

www.sandiegozoo.org takes visitors to the Center for Reproduction of Endangered Species (CRES) at the Zoological Society of San Diego, California. CRES is a research program dedicated to preserving and protecting rare and endangered wildlife. This site also has a link to the San Diego Zoo, whose Wild Animal Park contains more than 3,000 species of mammals, birds, and reptiles.

www.wildlifesafari.org is the official web site of the Wildlife Safari Park in Winston, Oregon. The African section of the park contains 85 acres (34 hectares) of open grassland with wooded areas, similar to the cheetah's natural habitat. Cheetahs, lions, zebras, and elephants live in the drive-through park.

Bibliography

These sources were useful to the author in researching this book. They provide interesting information about cheetahs for young readers who want to learn more.

Adamson, Joy. *Pippa's Challenge*. New York: Harcourt Brace Jovanovich, 1972.
   A true story based on Mrs. Adamson's experience with a hand-raised female cheetah in Kenya.

Bateman, Graham. *All the World's Animals: Carnivores*. New York: Torstar Books, 1984.
   A scientific and highly informative book about carnivores.

Conniff, Richard. "Cheetahs: Ghosts of the Grasslands." National Geographic 1966, no. 6 (December 1999): 2–31.
   A colorful description of the cheetahs and the people living in Namibia.

Index

Page numbers for illustrations are in **boldface**.

About the Author

GLORIA G. SCHLAEPFER shares her respect for the natural world through her writing, photography, and community activism. She has co-authored four books for children: *The African Rhinos*, *The Coyote*, *Pythons and Boas*, and *Bats*. Ms. Schlaepfer, who lives in Fullerton, California, has four children and four grandchildren.